MAR   2015

JOSEPH MIDTHUN   SAMUEL HITI

BUILDING BLOCKS OF SCIENCE

THE DIGESTIVE AND URINARY SYSTEMS

WORLD BOOK

a Scott Fetzer company
Chicago

www.worldbook.com

World Book, Inc.
233 N. Michigan Avenue
Chicago, IL 60601
U.S.A.

For information about other World Book publications,
visit our website at www.worldbook.com
or call 1-800-WORLDBK (967-5325).
For information about sales to schools and libraries,
call 1-800-975-3250 (United States),
or 1-800-837-5365 (Canada).

Library of Congress Cataloging-in-Publication Data

The digestive and urinary systems.
      pages cm. -- (Building blocks of science)
    Summary: "A graphic nonfiction volume that
introduces the digestive and urinary systems of
the human body"-- Provided by publisher.
   Includes index.
   ISBN 978-0-7166-1843-0
   1. Digestive organs--Juvenile literature. 2. Urinary
organs--Juvenile literature. I. World Book, Inc.
QP145.D53 2014
612.3--dc23
                              2013024691

Building Blocks of Science
ISBN: 978-0-7166-1840-9 (set, hc.)

Printed in China by Shenzhen Donnelley
Printing Co., Ltd., Guangdong Province
1st printing October 2013

Acknowledgments:
Created by Samuel Hiti and Joseph Midthun
Art by Samuel Hiti
Written by Joseph Midthun
Special thanks to Syril McNally

TABLE OF CONTENTS

There is a glossary on page 30. Terms defined in the glossary are in type **that looks like this** on their first appearance.

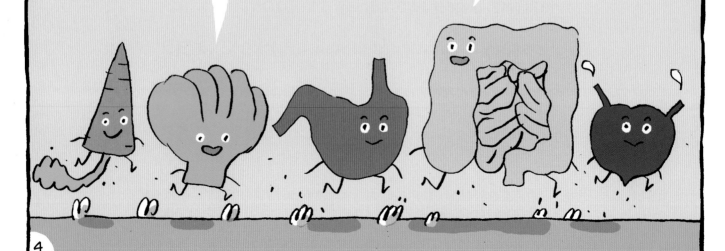

The human body is made up of trillions of tiny **cells**.

Each of these cells needs food to live.

Your digestive system breaks down food into pieces small enough for your cells to use.

As cells use food, they produce wastes.

These wastes must be removed from the body.

The **urinary system** includes the organs that work together to remove these wastes!

NUTRITION

Food contains many different chemicals.

But only a few dozen of these chemicals are needed to keep you healthy.

These few dozen are called **nutrients**.

Let's look at some of the main kinds of nutrients!

Proteins are one of the most important building blocks of the body.

They make up a large part of each cell in the body.

Your muscles and skin are mostly proteins.

Fats and carbohydrates provide energy.

Your body needs energy to run, walk, sit, sleep, and even think and digest.

Your body gets this energy by breaking down fats and carbohydrates, along with proteins.

Vitamins and minerals are needed for growing and repairing parts of the body.

They also take part in many chemical processes in the body. Each vitamin and mineral does a different job.

About two-thirds of your body is made up of water, a vital substance that helps keep your body working properly.

Your digestive system makes sure all of these nutrients get absorbed by the body so that they can be used!

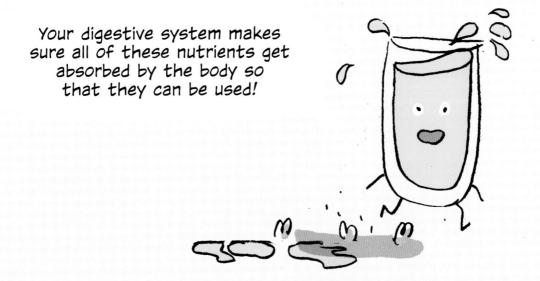

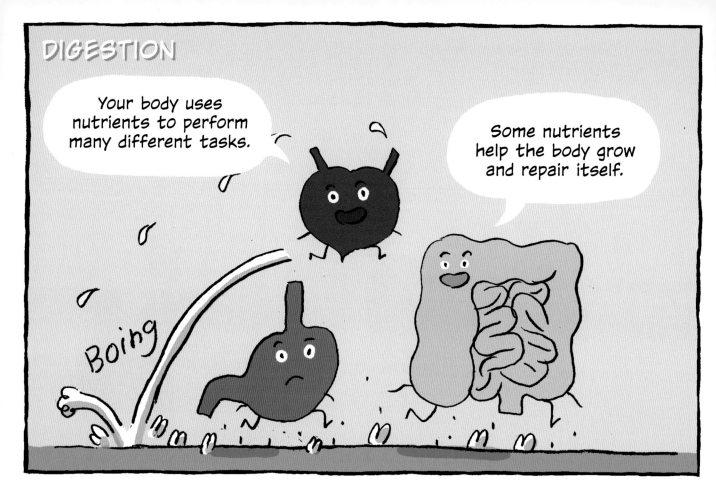

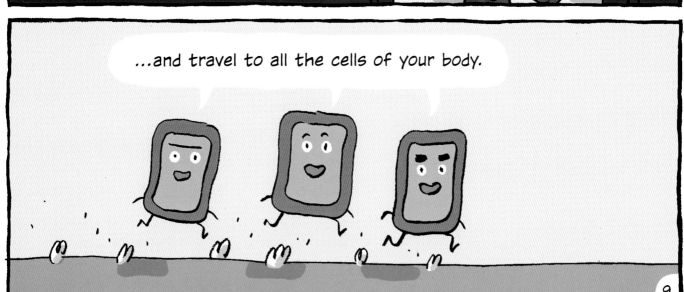

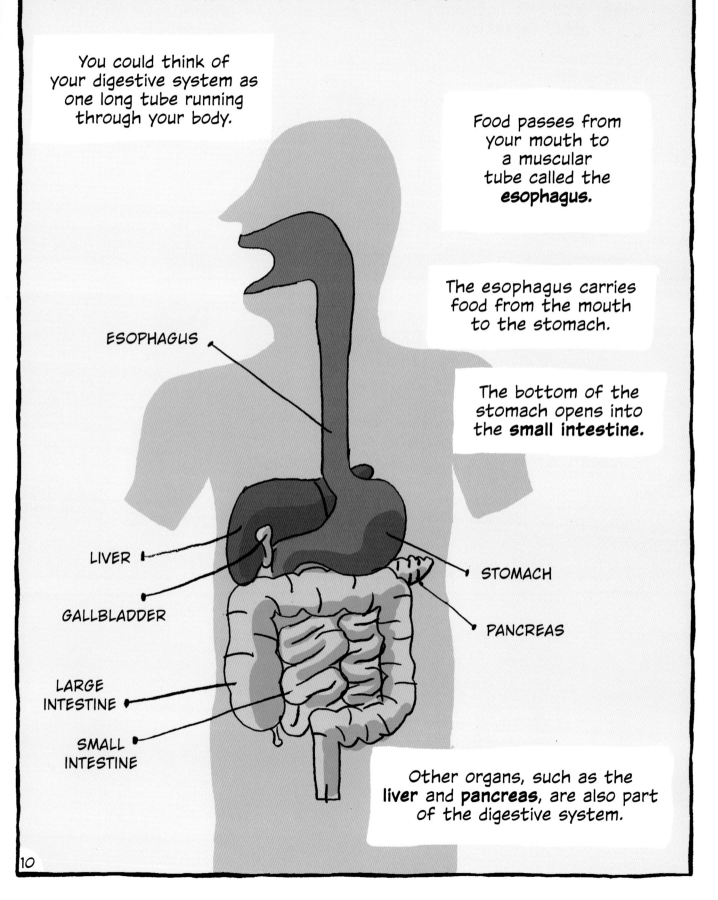

You could think of your digestive system as one long tube running through your body.

Food passes from your mouth to a muscular tube called the **esophagus.**

The esophagus carries food from the mouth to the stomach.

The bottom of the stomach opens into the **small intestine.**

ESOPHAGUS

LIVER

GALLBLADDER

LARGE INTESTINE

SMALL INTESTINE

STOMACH

PANCREAS

Other organs, such as the **liver** and **pancreas**, are also part of the digestive system.

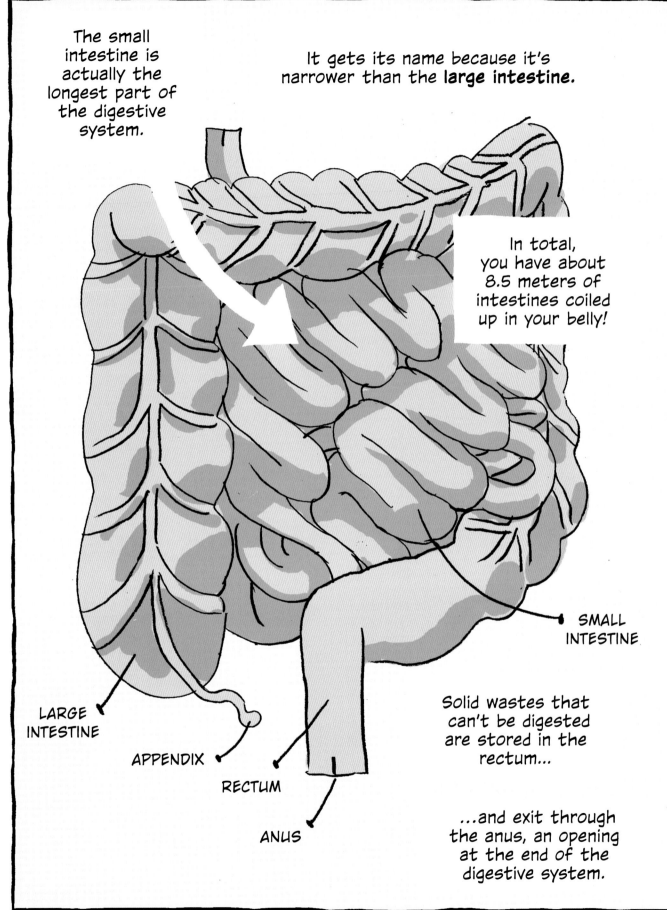

The small intestine is actually the longest part of the digestive system.

It gets its name because it's narrower than the **large intestine**.

In total, you have about 8.5 meters of intestines coiled up in your belly!

SMALL INTESTINE

LARGE INTESTINE

APPENDIX

RECTUM

ANUS

Solid wastes that can't be digested are stored in the rectum...

...and exit through the anus, an opening at the end of the digestive system.

THE MOUTH

Digestion begins when you take your first bite of food.

When you chew, your teeth break food into smaller and smaller pieces.

Your mouth also produces a liquid called saliva.

Saliva helps to break down a type of carbohydrate called starch.

HARD PALATE

NASAL CAVITY

SOFT PALATE

NOSTRIL

TONGUE

PHARYNX

EPIGLOTTIS

LARYNX

When you begin to swallow, the soft palate at the back of the mouth closes to keep food from going into the nasal passages.

TRACHEA

ESOPHAGUS

And a flap called the epiglottis closes to keep food from going down the trachea (windpipe) into the lungs.

TO THE RIGHT LUNG

TO THE LEFT LUNG

TO THE STOMACH

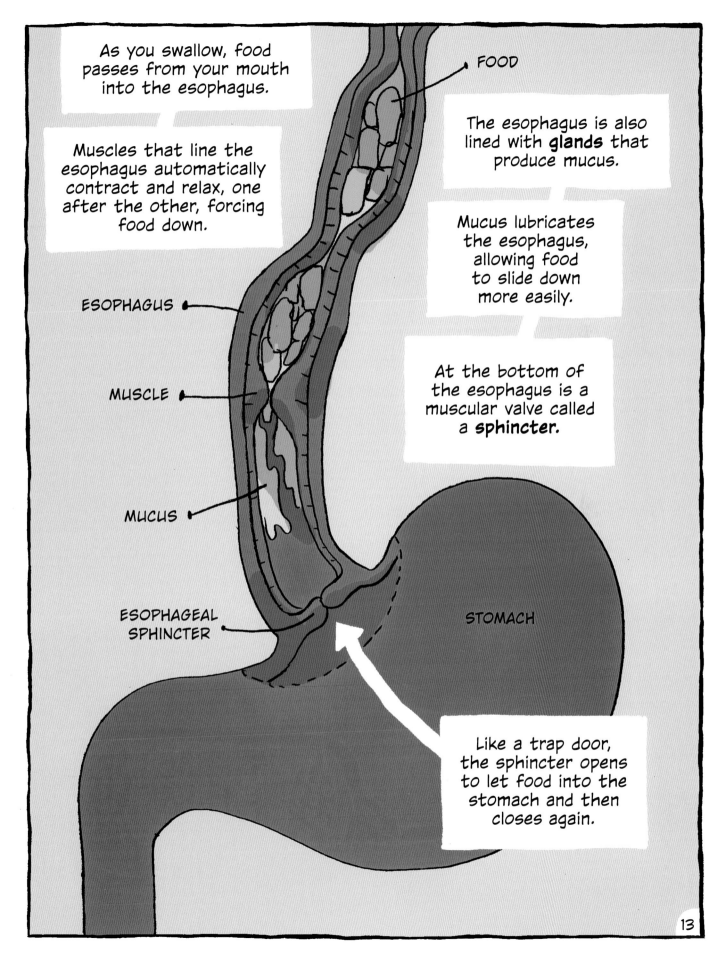

The stomach continues the digestive process by releasing chemicals that break down food.

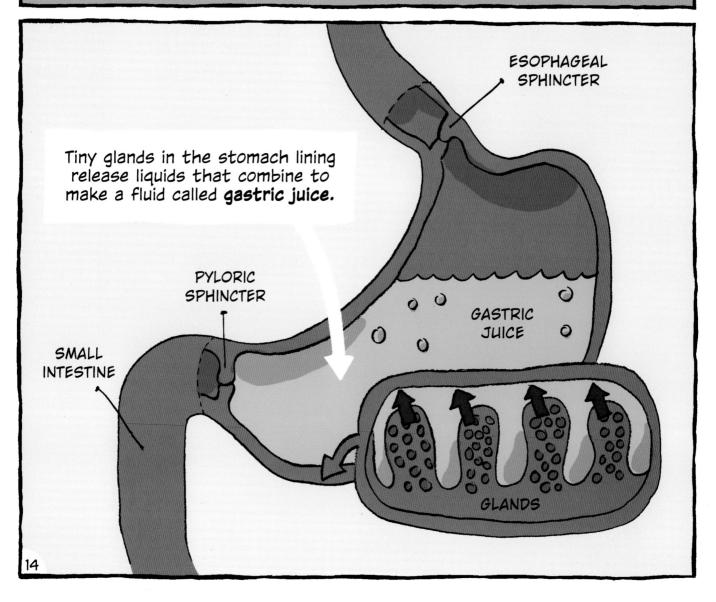

Tiny glands in the stomach lining release liquids that combine to make a fluid called **gastric juice.**

ESOPHAGEAL SPHINCTER

PYLORIC SPHINCTER

SMALL INTESTINE

GASTRIC JUICE

GLANDS

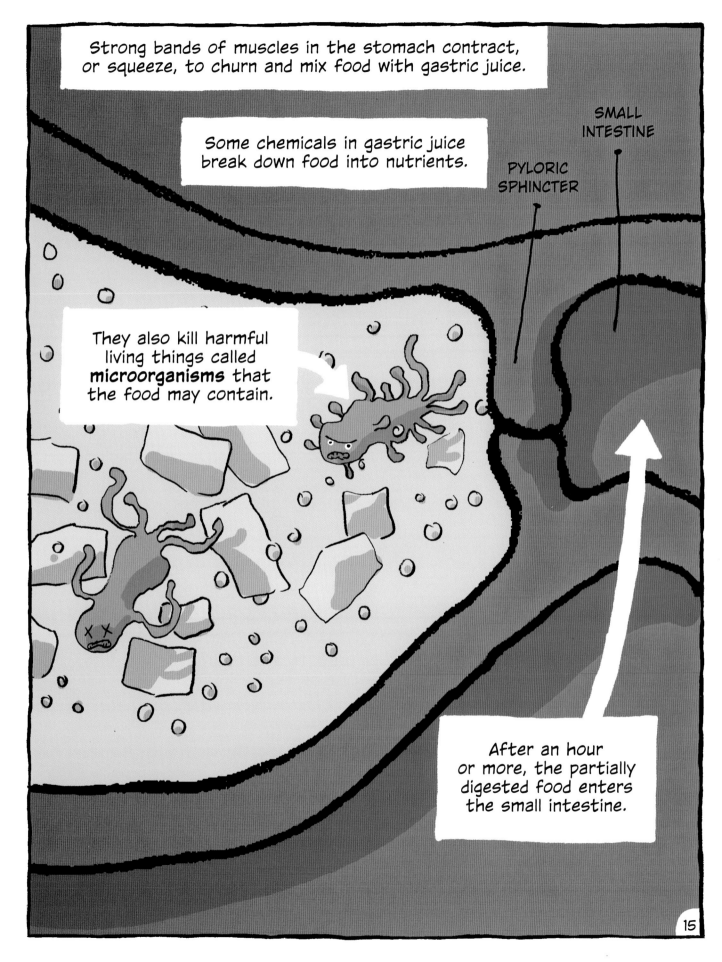

In the small intestine, partially digested food mixes with juices from several other organs.

These juices break down food even further.

The pancreas sends a juice that helps break down proteins.

The liver sends a greenish-yellow fluid called **bile,** which aids in the digestion of fats.

PANCREAS

LIVER

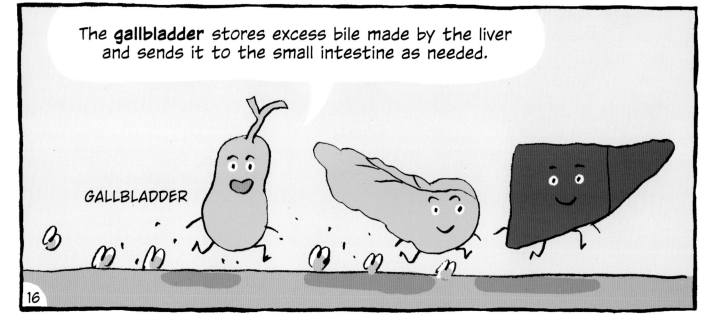

The **gallbladder** stores excess bile made by the liver and sends it to the small intestine as needed.

GALLBLADDER

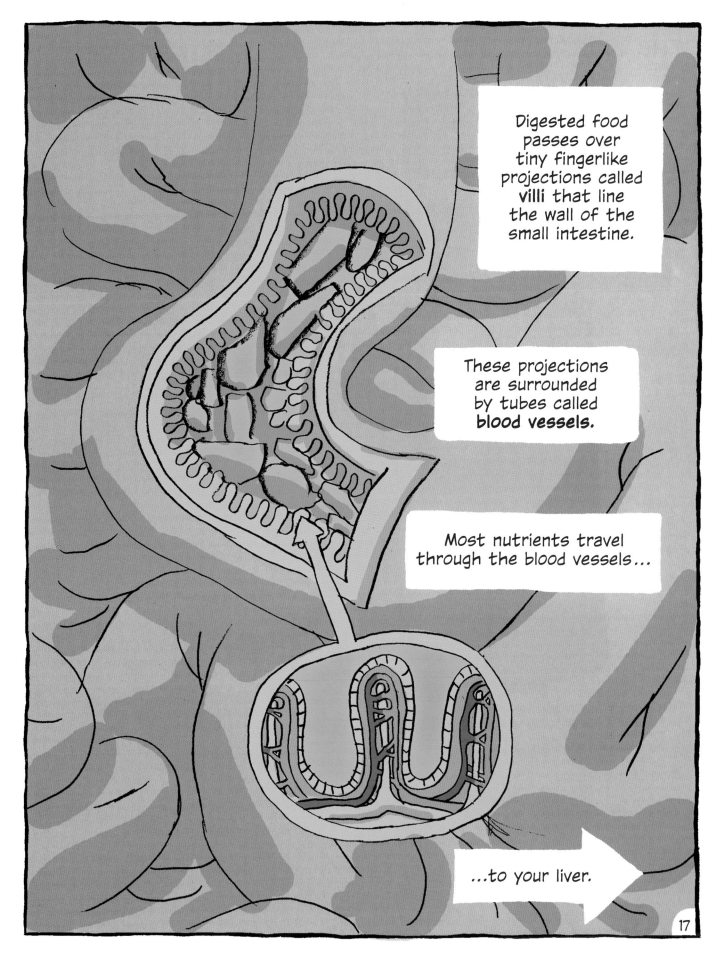

Digested food passes over tiny fingerlike projections called **villi** that line the wall of the small intestine.

These projections are surrounded by tubes called **blood vessels.**

Most nutrients travel through the blood vessels...

...to your liver.

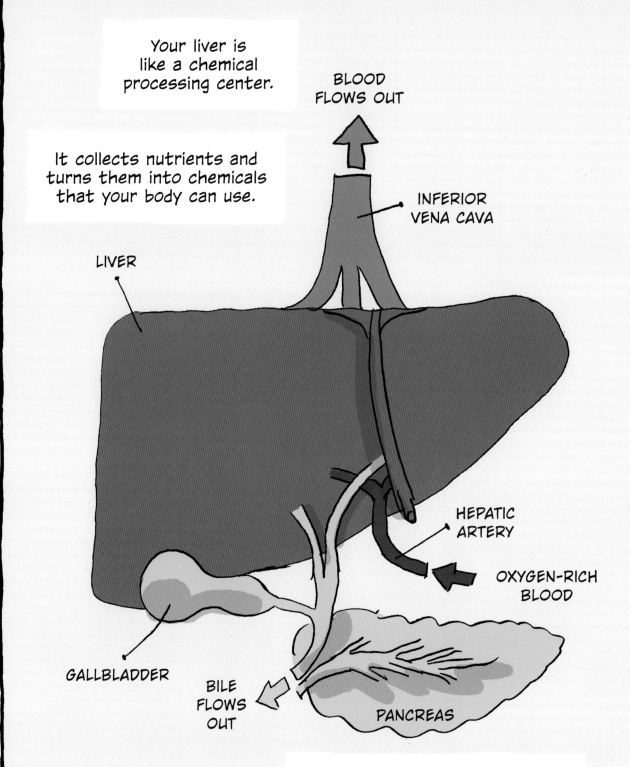

Your liver is like a chemical processing center.

It collects nutrients and turns them into chemicals that your body can use.

BLOOD FLOWS OUT

INFERIOR VENA CAVA

LIVER

HEPATIC ARTERY

OXYGEN-RICH BLOOD

GALLBLADDER

BILE FLOWS OUT

PANCREAS

It releases the chemicals into your bloodstream, where they travel to your cells.

Your small intestine carries out most of the digestive process.

The remaining undigested material moves to the large intestine...

...which absorbs water and salts from this material and eliminates the remaining waste from the body.

This waste is called feces.

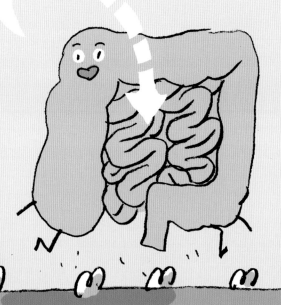

About two-thirds of feces is water.

The rest is solid material made up mostly of undigested plant fiber, **bacteria,** and other substances.

Feces are stored in the rectum until you go to toilet, when they are released through the anus.

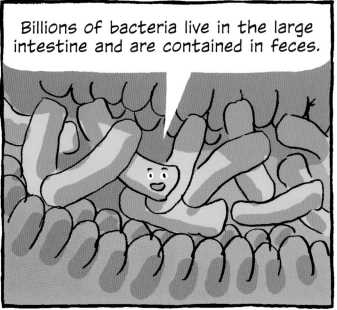

Billions of bacteria live in the large intestine and are contained in feces.

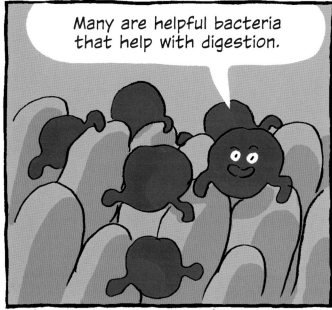

Many are helpful bacteria that help with digestion.

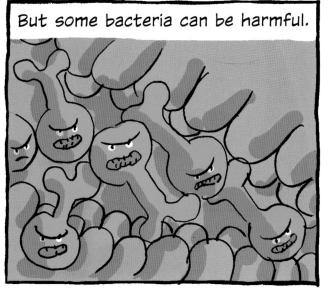

But some bacteria can be harmful.

That's why you should always wash your hands after you go to the bathroom!

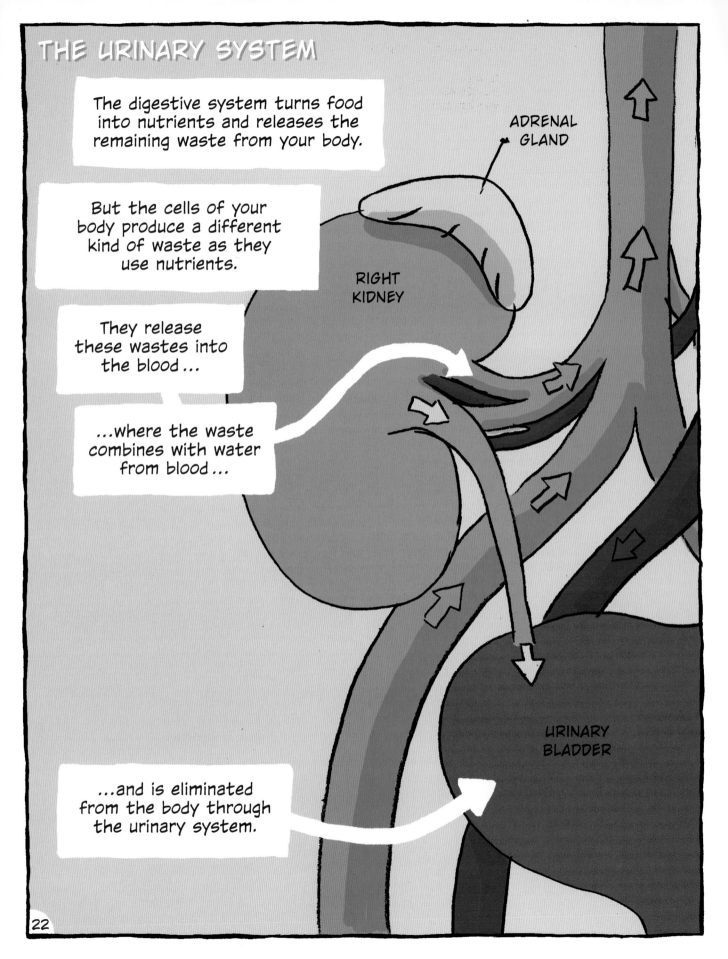

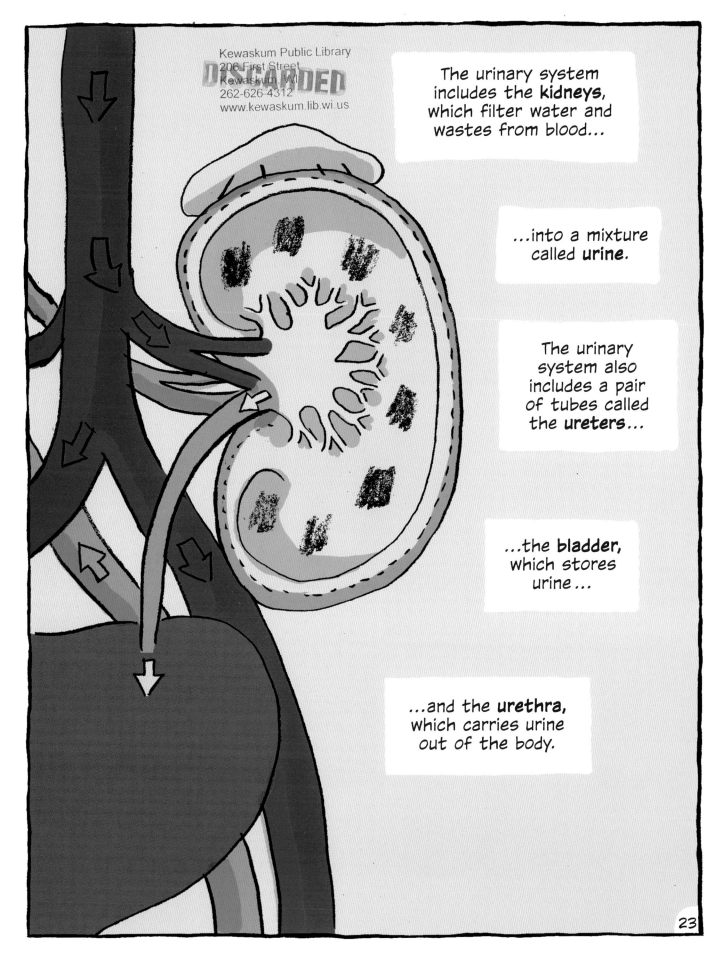

The urinary system includes the **kidneys**, which filter water and wastes from blood...

...into a mixture called **urine**.

The urinary system also includes a pair of tubes called the **ureters**...

...the **bladder**, which stores urine...

...and the **urethra**, which carries urine out of the body.

23

THE KIDNEYS

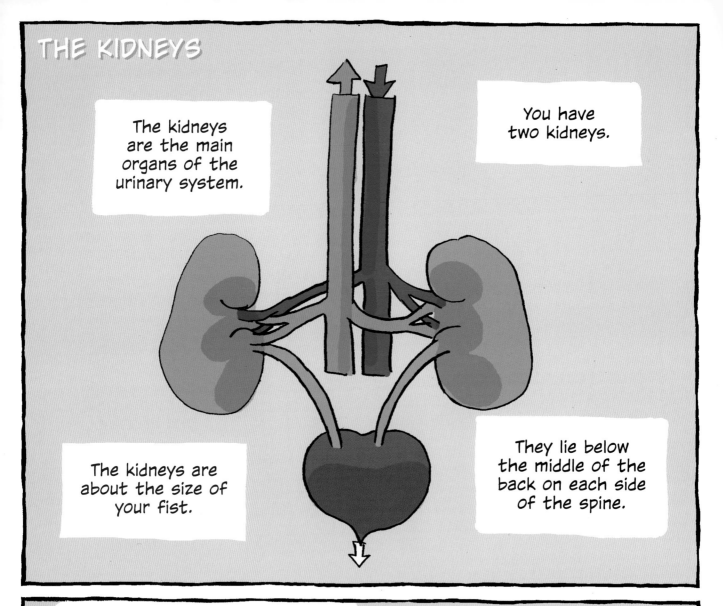

The kidneys are the main organs of the urinary system.

You have two kidneys.

The kidneys are about the size of your fist.

They lie below the middle of the back on each side of the spine.

Each kidney has millions of tiny structures that act as filters.

Blood passes through the filters.

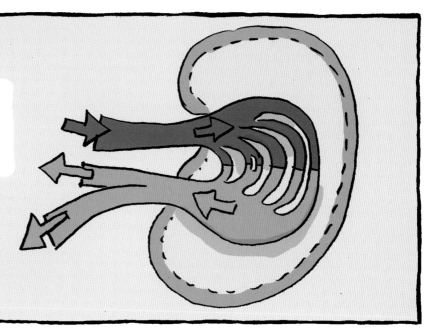

As it does, a network of tiny blood vessels removes water and other dissolved wastes.

The kidneys return some water and important chemicals to the body.

The remaining material makes up urine.

If the kidneys fail to function, poisons build up in the body, eventually causing death!

OOF!

TUMP

Hey, watch it!

THE URINARY TRACT

Urine from the kidneys flows out of the body along a system of tubes called the **urinary tract**.

This tract is made up of a ureter from each kidney, the bladder, and the urethra.

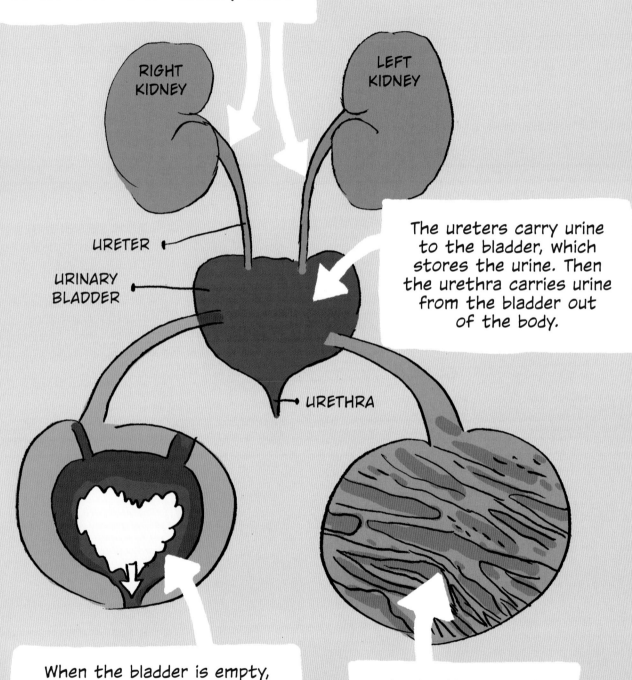

RIGHT KIDNEY

LEFT KIDNEY

URETER

URINARY BLADDER

URETHRA

The ureters carry urine to the bladder, which stores the urine. Then the urethra carries urine from the bladder out of the body.

When the bladder is empty, it is small and wrinkled.

The bladder is made up of muscle fibers.

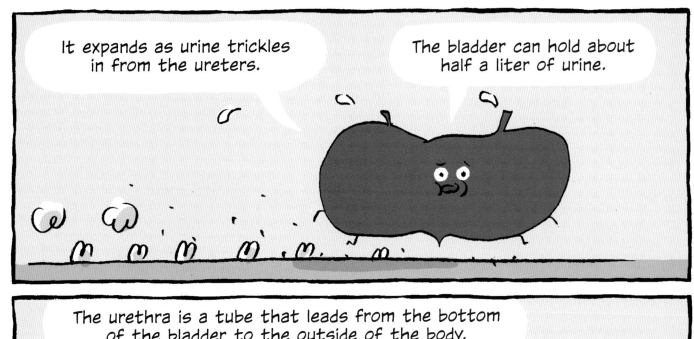

You have to look after your body to keep it working properly.

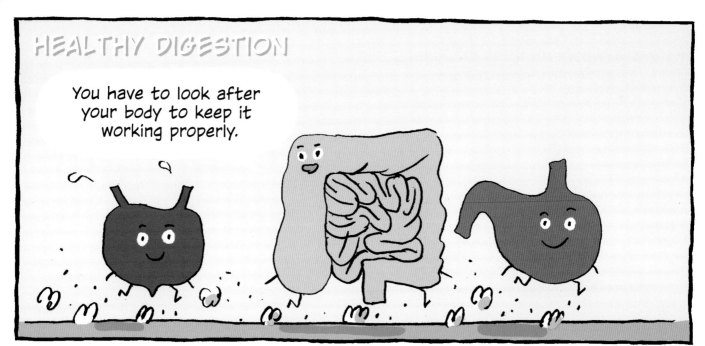

Drink plenty of water to keep both your digestive and urinary systems running smoothly!

Squirt

water

Roughage, also called dietary fiber, helps keep things moving through your digestive system.

GLOSSARY

bacterium; bacteria a tiny single-celled organism; more than one bacterium.

bile a greenish-yellow liquid made by the liver and stored in the gallbladder.

bladder a hollow organ that stores urine.

blood vessel a hollow tube that carries blood and nutrients through the body.

cell the basic unit of all living things.

digestion the process where food is broken down and absorbed by the body.

digestive system the group of organs that breaks down and absorbs food in the body.

esophagus a muscular tube connecting the mouth to the stomach.

gallbladder a small, saclike organ that stores digestive juices.

gastric juice digestive juice in the stomach that helps break down food molecules.

gland an organ that produces hormones or other substances.

kidney an organ that filters waste from the body to produce urine. The human body has two kidneys.

large intestine part of the digestive system that removes water and other materials from digested food.

liver an organ in the body that functions as a chemical factory and stores energy.

microorganism a tiny living thing.

molecule the smallest particle into which a substance can be divided and still have the chemical identity of the original substance.

nutrient a food substance that helps body growth.

organ two or more body tissues that work together to do a certain job.

pancreas an organ near the stomach that produces digestive juices and hormones.

small intestine an organ that breaks down and absorbs food.

sphincter a ringlike muscle that surrounds an opening of the body, and can contract to close it.

ureter a tube that carries urine from a kidney to the bladder.

urethra the tube where urine leaves the body.

urinary system the group of organs that removes wastes from the blood.

urinary tract the group of organs that remove wastes from the blood.

urine a yellowish fluid produced by the kidneys.

villi tiny fingerlike projections that line the wall of the small intestine.

FIND OUT MORE

Books

Digestive System
By Gretchen Hoffman
(Benchmark Books, 2008)

Guts: Our Digestive System
by Seymour Simon
(HarperCollins, 2005)

Human Body
by Richard Walker
(DK Children, 2009)

Human Body Factory: The Nuts and Bolts of Your Insides
by Dan Green
(Kingfisher, 2012)

Start Exploring: Gray's Anatomy: A Fact-Filled Coloring Book
by Freddy Stark
(Running Press Kids, 2011)

The Digestive System
by Christine Taylor-Butler
(Children's Press, 2008)

The Dynamic Digestive System: How Does My Stomach Work?
by John Burstein
(Crabtree, 2009)

The Quest to Digest
by Mary K. Corcoran
(Charlesbridge Publishing, 2010)

The Way We Work
by David Macaulay
(Houghton Mifflin/Walter Lorraine Books, 2008)

Websites

Discovery Kids: Your Digestive System
http://kids.discovery.com/tell-me/science/body-systems/your-digestive-system
Get an in-depth education on all of the parts that make up the digestive system, fun facts included!

E-Learning for Kids: The Digestive System
http://www.e-learningforkids.org/Courses/Liquid_Animation/Body_Parts/Digestive_System/
Take a peek inside your digestive system in this clickable lesson with bonus comprehension exercises.

Kids Biology: Digestive System
http://www.kidsbiology.com/human_biology/digestive-system.php
Learn all about the digestive system by watching a short video and reading fact-filled articles complete with images of the body's organs.

Kids Health: How the Body Works
http://kidshealth.org/kid/htbw/
Select a body part to watch a video, play a word find, or read an article to learn more about its function in the human body.

Kids.Net.Au: Digestive System
http://encyclopedia.kids.net.au/page/di/Digestive_system
All of your questions about the digestive system will be answered in this description of one of your body systems.

NeoK12: Digestive System
http://www.neok12.com/Digestive-System.htm
Watch videos that illustrate the flow of the digestive system, and then take grade-specific quizzes to test your knowledge.

Science Kids: Human Body for Kids
http://www.sciencekids.co.nz/humanbody.html
Sample a range of educational games, challenging experiments, and mind-bending quizzes all while learning about human body topics.

INDEX